DBT Skills Workbook for Teens

101 Engaging Exercises and Activities for Handling Difficult Emotions, Increasing Awareness, and Enhancing Coping Skills

Table of Contents

Letter to Parents

Dear Parents,

Thank you for taking the first step toward showing interest in your child's mental health. With the advent of social media and other pressures, it can be difficult for a teenager to navigate the world. Moreover, it is frustrating for you to connect with your child at this volatile stage in their life. However, persevering through frustration will be rewarding when your child's mental health is optimum.

Have patience. The journey will be long, awkward, and adventurous, but the outcomes are worth it. Applying DBT methods allows teenagers to better navigate their emotions and interpersonal relationships to understand themselves and their place in the world. Be open to communicating with your teen along this road. With your help, the positive results of DBT can be applied. Furthermore, you could apply some techniques for yourself because mental health is a lifelong journey.

You are encouraged to make this book a collaborative effort with your child using openness and honesty. The global mental health crisis among teenagers in the modern world is concerning. Interventions are needed to ensure the positive well-being of children is the first consideration.

Letter to Teenagers

Dear Teens,

Life seems to be coming at you quickly in the teenage transition phase. The bridge from adolescence to adulthood can be extremely overwhelming at times. Your challenges can be debilitating, but you do not have to go through them blindly. By being proactive in understanding your emotions, behaviors, and interpersonal relationships on a deeper level, you can gain the superpower of awareness and the ability to respond consciously in any scenario.

DBT gives you the tools to understand yourself through introspective examination while gaining the ability to manage your emotions and strengthen your relationships. You are now stamping your signature on the world while shaping your impact on society. So, thank you for taking yourself seriously enough to be proactive in improving yourself by adjusting key aspects of engaging with yourself and the world.

With the mindfulness, emotional regulation, distress control, and interpersonal effectiveness this DBT workbook offers, you will understand yourself, your habits, your emotions, and your motivations more profoundly. The self-directed activities and exercises in this book put your internal environment in your hands, allowing you to navigate the external environment, maximizing the benefits of this information at your fingertips.

Section 1: Understanding DBT and Its Many Benefits

To implement DBT strategies and therapeutic approaches effectively, it is necessary first to gain an in-depth understanding of the framework and how it is used in various contexts. Therefore, the first section of this workbook provides a theoretical background to the exercises within these pages. A background understanding of DBT will help rationalize the exercises by clearly illustrating what you will gain if you implement and internalize these activities.

What Is DBT?

DBT is an acronym for "Dialectical Behavior Therapy." The DBT therapeutic approach is cognitive behavioral therapy, which gives you the tools to manage your emotions, conduct yourself interpersonally in a healthy way, and develop effective coping mechanisms by staying in the present moment. The approach was developed to treat people with Borderline Personality Disorder, or BPD. Still, it is effective for anyone looking to better self-regulate, minimizing self-destructive behaviors like addiction or eating disorders.

The Benefits of DBT as a Therapeutic Approach

The benefits of DBT come from *radical acceptance*. By accepting reality as it is, including the past, present, and future's possible limitations, decisions can be made more consciously. Establishing yourself at the moment to clearly and honestly analyze yourself is a foundation to correct detrimental behavior. Furthermore, you can amplify your strengths by knowing how your good decisions have led to positive outcomes.

The History and Foundation of DBT

DBT has sprung from cognitive behavioral therapy (CBT) and, therefore, is considered a type of CBT. Initially, the DBT framework was clinically trialed on individuals with high suicidal tendencies and those with borderline personality disorder. At first, therapists used DBT as a problem-solving mechanism. However, practitioners discovered that directly addressing problems through a narrow view felt *alienating* to clients. Therefore, DBT was further developed to systematically analyze

---

behavioral patterns and the person's current position to introduce gradual change.

The Pillars of DBT

DBT can be broken down into four core components or pillars: emotional regulation, interpersonal effectiveness, mindfulness, and distress tolerance. If each word of DBT is broken down, it becomes clear how these four corners form the foundation of dialectical behavioral therapy. The word "dialectical" refers to a logical investigation of ideas or concepts by contrasting different aspects of the explored topic. This examination involves the introspection of your motivations, thought patterns, and behaviors in a therapeutic setting. By getting to the root of your decisions using various techniques, DBT can create meaningful change in your life.

Emotional Regulation

For most people, emotional responses are automatic. It isn't easy to control your reaction to a situation. However, what can be controlled is the route you take after experiencing an emotion. DBT allows you to enter the present moment with knowledge of your past to intervene and intercept behavioral patterns detrimental to you and others. Experiencing emotions, identifying your triggers, and developing healthy emotional management mechanisms help you regulate feelings.

Interpersonal Effectiveness

If you understand your emotions and motivations, you are well-equipped interpersonally. Interpersonal effectiveness means setting and enforcing strong boundaries and knowing how to say "no." Moreover, DBT allows you to look at the dynamics of past and present relationships to measure what works and what hinders you. Understanding yourself in relation to others can help you navigate relationships and social interactions more knowledgeably.

Mindfulness

Mindfulness is the art of being present. People miss a lot when they excessively dwell on the past and imagine their future. Mindfulness practices bring you into the present moment so you can move on from what you can do right now. Change does not come with one big step but rather with the small decisions you make daily.

Distress Tolerance

The last thing you want is a distressing situation spiraling you into an even worse position. Small disasters become massive if you do not have the right tools for distress tolerance. Crises will inevitably appear at your doorstep regardless of how much you try to avoid them. Therefore, self-soothing methods and finding non-destructive distractions are key to dealing with distressing moments.

The Effectiveness and Adaptability of DBT Strategies

As a teenager, you are in a transition phase from adolescence into adulthood. Therefore, the importance of managing emotions becomes more apparent. One technique used in the DBT framework to manage emotions is consciously feeling your emotions. For instance, a distressing situation occurs, like someone embarrassing you in the classroom. Ask yourself questions like how intense the emotion is, what triggered the feeling, and what steps you can take to ease your discomfort. It allows you to take a moment to act rationally instead of being impulse-driven.

Peer pressure is often framed as a teen issue. However, the human drive to socially connect makes peer pressure a reality that continues throughout life. With DBT's mindfulness practices and the introspection it promotes, peer pressure can be deconstructed, allowing you to determine whether following the crowd benefits your present and future self. In this way, you will not fall victim to following the group flow but will follow with awareness.

Since navigating social spaces requires communication skills, DBT provides effective communication tools. Understanding yourself and your motivations gives you the courage to set strict boundaries. For example, your friend calls you to play video games, but you know you have an assignment due. If you have clearly defined goals for what you want to achieve in the assignment, you will draw a boundary on your time and refuse the invitation.

Section 2: The Magic of Mindfulness

Mindfulness sometimes has a bad reputation as something for woo-woo hippies with crystals, beads, and incense. However, scientifically-backed data suggests that mindfulness can be therapeutic. The various practices mindfulness encompasses help reduce stress, improve focus, and positively contribute to your overall emotional well-being. Mindfulness is an anchor to reality when your mind runs away with you.

Mindfulness is bringing yourself into the current moment to observe your inner state and your surroundings free from judgment. DBT is based on observing and understanding your emotions so that you can react to them in ways that benefit you most. Mindfulness allows you to be present enough to pause and analyze your emotions before you automatically react. With mindfulness, you can measure your emotional temperature to know how to use your feelings instead of letting them control you.

Mindfulness Exercises

Exercise 1: Aligning with the Now

Meditation is the foundation of mindfulness. Many meditation techniques exist, and most are centered on breathing. Therefore, begin your mindfulness journey by sitting in a comfortable, cross-legged position with your spine straight. Set a timer for 10 minutes. Now, breathe in through your nostrils and out through your mouth. Focus on your breathing. Thoughts will flow into your mind. Do not judge your thoughts; simply allow them to flow while focusing on your breath. It will usher you into the present moment.

Meditating in the lotus pose can guide you into the present moment.
https://www.pexels.com/photo/a-woman-doing-a-meditation-on-a-beach-during-morning-8964915/

Exercise 2: The Room Game

Mindfulness is making yourself aware of the present moment. An easy exercise to implement daily is listing what you see when you enter a room. Enter into your bedroom. Make a list in your mind of everything you see. Do this at least once a day as you enter your bedroom. This exercise can be done anywhere when you feel anxious; simply make a list in your mind of everything you see in the room.

Exercise 3: Mindfulness Coloring

Coloring is a great exercise for mindfulness. Gather colored pens, pencils, or highlighters and color in the details of the mandala below. Take time to color all the intricate details. Allow your mind to become fully focused on the coloring task. Preferably color the image in a quiet room so your focus is maximized.

Exercise 4: Body Scan

Emotions and stress are often stored in various body parts. After a long day, you may feel tension in your back or shoulders. Therefore, a meditational body scan could help you identify pressure points and use your body as a vehicle to understand your emotional state. To perform a general meditation body scan, start by lying down comfortably. Take a few deep breaths, slowly releasing your breath through your nose. Once completely calm, imagine a white light slowly moving from your toes to your head. Note how that section of your body feels as it passes over each body part. Note which emotions are attached to the body parts where you feel pain or discomfort. Breathe deeply into the discomfort and exhale to relieve the pain. You can do this cycle as many times as necessary.

Exercise 5: Environment Visualization

Visualization is a significant part of mindfulness, but other senses also get involved, like hearing. Go outside to a park or even into a busy public area. Sit on a bench and write down all the sounds you hear for about thirty minutes. Visit the same place about five times and note how each time you visit, the sounds differ.

Exercise 6: Washing Away Your Worries

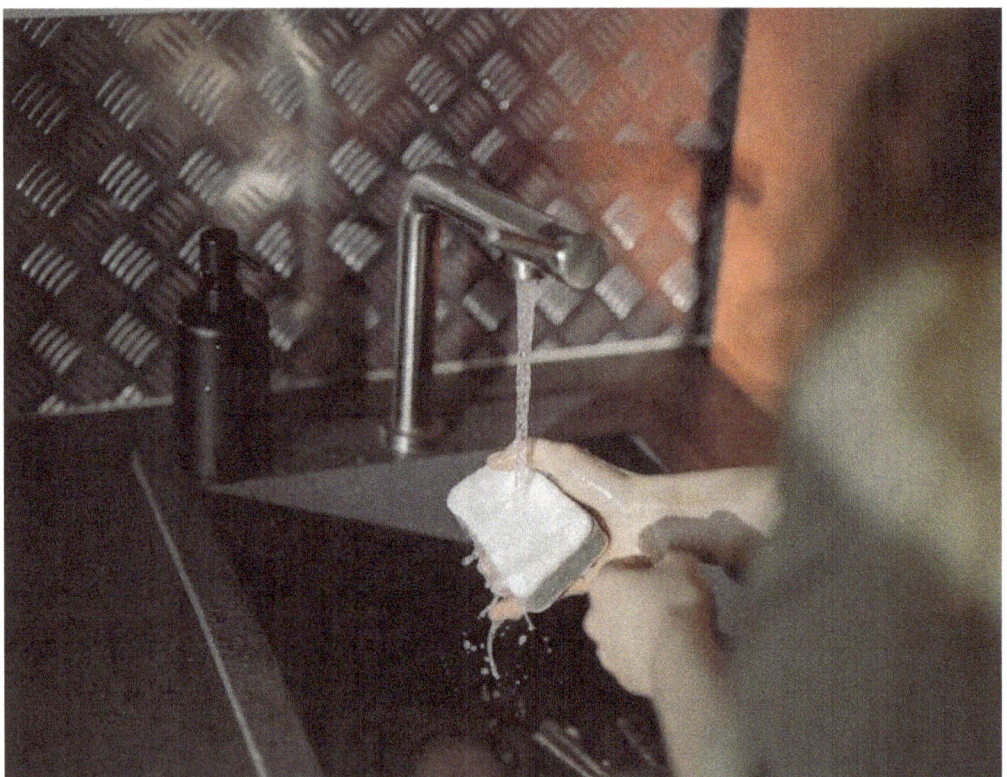

Doing dishes can bring you to the present moment.
https://www.pexels.com/photo/person-holding-white-paper-near-stainless-steel-faucet-4108680/

Chores can bring you to the present moment. For instance, take time to wash the dishes. Do not use distractions like music or YouTube videos while washing the dishes. Note the various textures you feel, like the soap, the plates, and the cutlery. Mentally examine all the details, like the water temperature and how it makes your hands feel.

Exercise 7: Mindful Eating

Eating can become a mindfulness exercise. It is similar to what critics or judges on cooking shows do. Set up a platter of various foods. It doesn't need to be fancy. It can be a plate with two or three types of fruit and some crackers. Pay close attention to what you are eating. Notice the texture on your fingers and in your mouth. Note the aromas and tastes. Eat slowly and consciously. This exercise can be done with any meal.

Exercise 8: Walking Meditation

Walking meditation is greatly beneficial for increasing focus and stimulating relaxation. Find a path with different sections forming it, like a quiet sidewalk, a brick walkway, or tiles. Set a timer for five minutes. Create a pattern in your mind from the bricks, wood, tiles, or whatever material the walkway is made from. Walk along the pattern repeatedly without rushing, carefully noticing the placement of your feet.

Exercise 9: Planting Your Presentness

Gardening can help you connect with nature.
https://www.pexels.com/photo/person-digging-on-soil-using-garden-shovel-1301856/

Gardening is the perfect mindful grounding exercise. Participate in awareness gardening - being barefoot can truly enhance the exercise. Feel the earth beneath your feet and the soil in between your fingers. Examine the various plant textures, acknowledging how the weather and temperature make you feel. Take in the sounds and smells while you tend to the garden.

Exercise 10: Mantras of Mindfulness

This breathing and mantra exercise helps if you are experiencing anxiety. When you begin feeling anxious, take slow, deep breaths. Use these affirmations with each exhale.

- "I am Calm."
- "I am Safe."
- "I am Whole."
- "I am filled with Power."
- "I am an Overcomer."

Run through this cycle until you feel your anxious thoughts subsiding.

Exercise 11: Pause and Process

When angry, use this mindfulness exercise to prevent an impulsive response. Pause and take a few deep breaths. Ask yourself, "Why am I feeling angry?" Then, ask yourself, "What is the worst course of action I could take?" Lastly, ask yourself, "What can I do now to reduce my anger and address my discomfort?" This pause helps you examine your emotions and prevents you from making irrational spur-of-the-moment decisions.

Exercise 12: Positivity Breathing

A simple activity to help if you are feeling down is positivity breathing. Sit in a comfortable position. Imagine a cord connected to a gigantic ball of golden comforting sunshine going from your chest. When you breathe in, imagine the positivity from the ball traveling through the cord filling your body. When you breathe out, imagine the positivity that has filled your body, pushing all the negativity out via your exhale.

Section 3: Labeling and Recognizing Your Feelings

Humans understand the world using pattern recognition and categorizing. Considering that DBT is meant to allow you to better understand and accept difficult feelings, labeling your emotions can provide you with a logical way to examine yourself using boxes to neatly sort your emotions into. Furthermore, labeling your feelings is an exercise aligned with mindfulness because describing what you are feeling in the moment brings you into a present awareness of yourself.

Sometimes, emotions get framed in your mind as positive or negative. People say, I feel good, or I feel bad. It is a simplistic way of looking at the array of emotions people are capable of experiencing. Therefore, DBT exercises help identify and more deeply understand your feelings. These exercises help you to facilitate mental wellness from an informed space and help you develop decision-making skills.

DBT Exercises to Identify Your Feelings

Exercise 13: Describing What You Feel

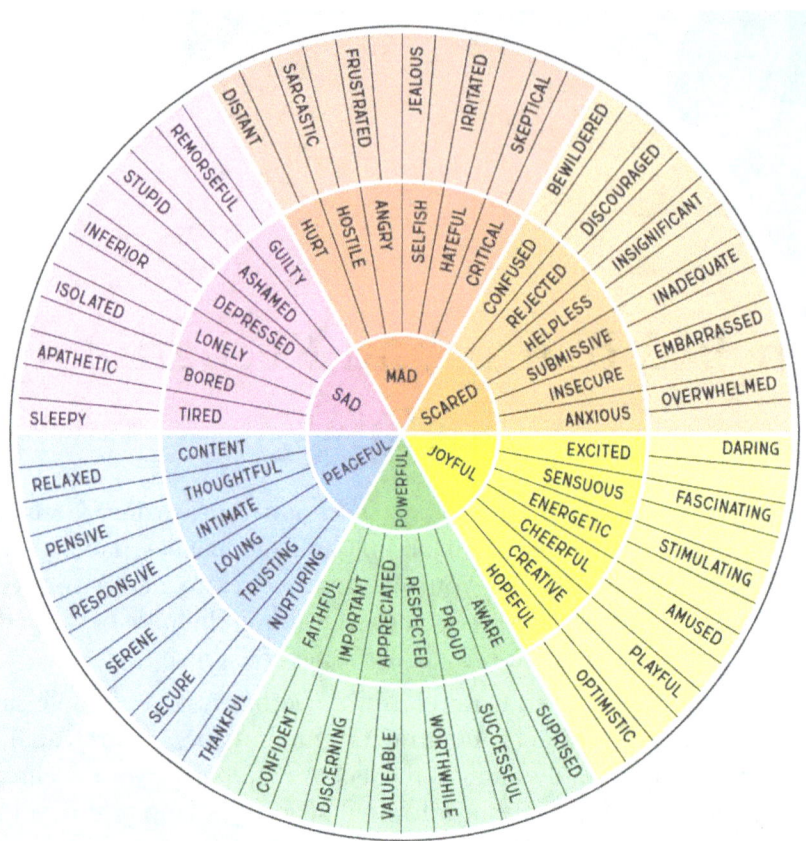

The first place to start identifying emotions and developing emotional awareness is by labeling your feelings beyond merely bad or good.

Here's a list of emotions to describe your feelings:

Positive: joyful, excited, blissful, relieved, secure, fulfilled, loved, interested, pleased, content.

Negative: nervous, vengeful, shy, guilty, jealous, bored, depressed, antagonistic, regretful, angry.

Exercise 14: The Emotions Scale

After labeling your emotions, determining how positively or negatively you perceive the emotion is useful. You can do this by weighing your emotions on the following scale:

Exercise 15: Emotional Intensity Scale

Once you determine how negatively or positively the emotions impact you, use a similar scale to measure the emotion's intensity. It helps you find the most appropriate reaction method and determines each emotional experience's importance.

Exercise 16: Journaling to Greatness

Now that you have the vocabulary to label your emotions, the scales to measure the intensity, and your emotion's positive or negative impact, you can begin journaling. The first thing in the morning, when you wake up, write down how you feel and your expectations for the day ahead. Also, include your dreams from the night before. Then, the last thing before bed, write about your experiences during the day and how they made you feel.

Exercise 17: Draw Your Feelings

Some people are not linguistically inclined, so it becomes challenging to write about your emotions. Draw an image of how you feel. It can be as abstract and chaotic as you want, but ensure it reflects your feelings. By drawing your emotions, you can more deeply analyze how you feel at the moment or about a particular occurrence.

Exercise 18: Negative Emotion Tunnel

Sometimes, a situation can create adverse emotions. These emotions could stem from feeling like you do not have control. This exercise helps you navigate the emotion of helplessness. Firstly, describe your situation. Now imagine the absolute worst thing that could happen due to the situation. Once you have created the worst-case scenario, imagine the best outcome resulting from the situation. Once you have both images in mind, decide the best course of action to get you closer to the ideal.

Exercise 19: Feel Your Emotions

People seldom allow themselves to simply feel their emotions. Feeling is one of the best practices you can implement for emotional regulation. The next time you feel a negative emotion, instead of trying to suppress or change the emotion, just sit down by yourself and allow it to flow. Do not judge the emotion or the accompanying thoughts. Merely sit and observe them.

Exercise 20: Identifying Emotional Patterns

Becoming mindful of your emotional patterns gives you more power in emotional regulation. This exercise takes a few weeks. Every day for a month, write down the main emotions you felt daily. Review the emotions you felt at the end of the month and see what patterns emerge. By recording your emotions and observing trends, you will realize habitual behaviors causing negativity. From this standpoint, you can make the necessary adjustments to your behavior.

Exercise 21: Run and Return

Going for a run can reduce the intensity of your emotions
https://www.pexels.com/photo/selective-focus-photography-of-woman-in-pink-shirt-1199590/

Sometimes, a distraction is necessary to process emotions. Walking away from emotion and intending to revisit it later can be eye-opening. If you are overwhelmed with emotion, go for a 30-minute run. It will get your heart pumping and reduce the emotion's intensity.

Exercise 22: Angle Your Perception

Emotional distress is not always caused by an event, but it can result from your interpretation of an event – or your "angle." Therefore, take time to think about how you feel about a certain event. After identifying your feelings, ask yourself why you felt that way. Once the "why" is answered, recognize this is an interpretation of reality. It may not be as you perceive it. Put yourself in other people's shoes and imagine different interpretations of the event. It can provide deeper insight and clarity to many emotional reactions.

Exercise 23: Shout It Out

Part of the DBT approach to emotional regulation is allowing yourself to feel and express yourself emotionally. Often, the pressure of life can become too much. A way to release the pressure valve is by going to a secluded area and letting out a deep belly shout or scream. This directionless expression of emotion can truly allow you to feel with the involvement of your voice.

Exercise 24: Beat Out Your Aggression

A great way to regulate aggression is by expressing it so it is not harmful to others. Get a pillow, and with a baseball bat, beat it until you feel better. Yell your frustrations at the pillow and allow that channel for release.

Section 4: Dialectics: Balancing Thoughts and Emotions

Dialectics is a philosophical exercise where the extremes of two viewpoints are allowed to exist simultaneously to investigate missing parts of the picture or to find a middle ground. Since "dialectical" is the first word in Dialectical Behavioral Therapy, using dialectics is central to DBT. Looking at both sides of the coin, a happy medium could be found in the middle. Extremities are where irrationalities are planted. Therefore, you could create a more balanced mental state by weighing opposing views to find a central meeting place.

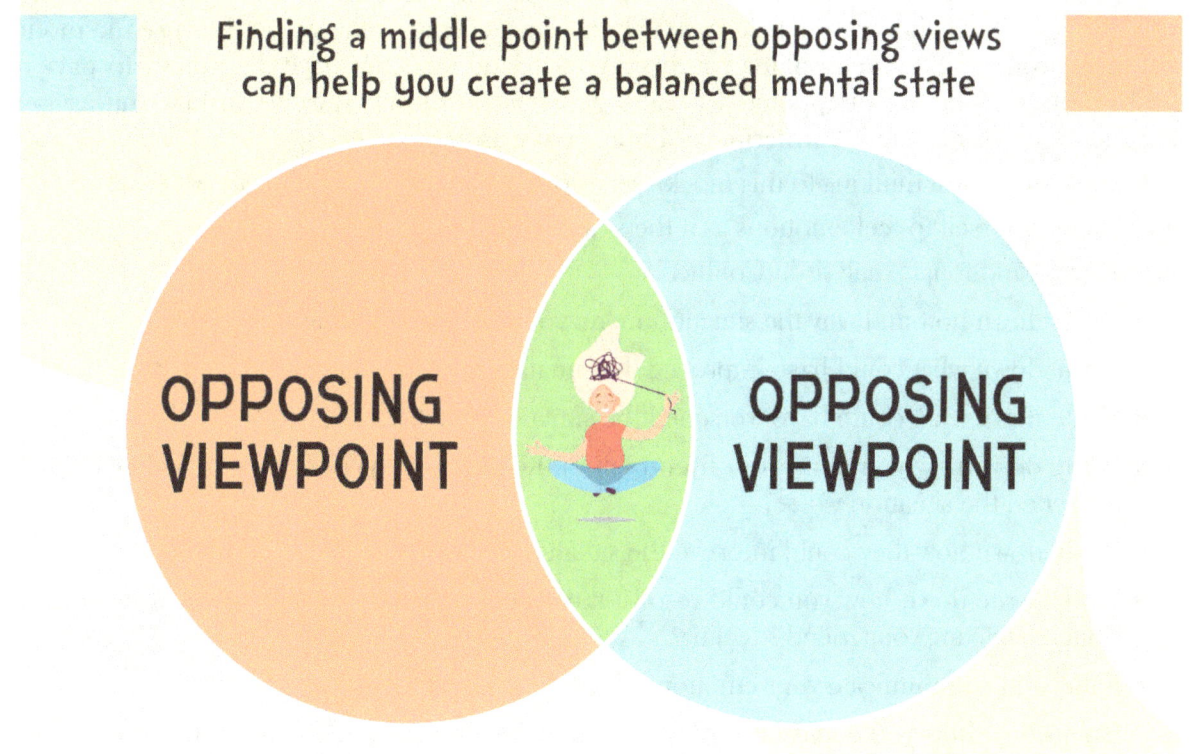

How to Balance Thoughts and Emotions

Exercise 25: Marking a Switch in Behavior

This exercise will help you contrast your current behavior with your desired behavior to determine what changes and adaptations you can make to achieve your preferred outcome.

- Write down where you want to see yourself in the next five years and where you currently are.
- Then, write down what prevents you from getting to where you want to be. Next, write down what will help you get where you want to be.
- Lastly, write down what you are doing to get you where you want to be and what hinders you from achieving your goal.

Dialectical Analysis for Conflict Resolution

Exercise 26: Putting On Another's Shoes

When you have a conflict with a friend and want to resolve the situation, consider how the situation makes you feel. Now consider how it makes your friend feel. Imagine what your friend could do to improve the situation. Now imagine what you can do to improve the situation. Lastly, imagine what you could do to worsen the situation and what your friend could do to worsen it. You can find a clearer view of the conflict from these contrasting points of analysis.

Exercise 27: Dialectic Conflict Resolution

Here's a mock example of how you can solve a conflict by using the dialectic approach. For instance, you and your friend are saving money together to buy a videogame console or another expensive item you are both interested in. Every month, you put aside money your friend keeps at home. Your friend's brother gets locked up in jail on a misdemeanor charge, so they use the money to bail out their brother without consulting you first. Your friend does not have the money to pay you to replenish the fund. You are disappointed because your friend didn't consult you first and aggravated because the money is depleted. Furthermore, a breach of trust has occurred.

Now, apply dialectical thinking to this mock scenario.

Firstly, allow yourself to feel emotions as if the situation had occurred.

Exercise 28: Emotional Analysis in Conflict

- Write down how and why the situation made you feel a certain way.
- Write down what could have improved the situation.
- Write down what could have worsened the situation worse.
- Write down how you think your friend felt in the situation. Write down how they could have worsened the situation worse.
- Write down how they could improve the situation better.
- Lastly, write down how you could resolve the conflict. Include ways to assert your boundaries while respecting your friend's feelings.
- Label and communicate your emotions clearly.
- Brainstorm how you could have prevented the situation from happening and how you would approach similar situations.

Writing down how you feel can be therapeutic and help you organize your thoughts.

Working on Your Emotional Intelligence

Exercise 29: The Paradox Game

Increasing your emotional intelligence requires holding space for paradoxical opposite realities about yourself. Write a list of at least ten feelings or actions that you seem in conflict or oppositional. For example, "I am courageous, but I am scared of rats," or "I am lazy, but I study hard for tests." This exercise can be practiced every day. You can write a few of these dialectical statements or push yourself to see how many you can come up with in one sitting. It will help you compare two opposing ideas and determine how they can co-exist.

Exercise 30: Opposing Views of Conflict

Imagine your parent or guardian asking you to clean the house before they get home. You have extra classes after school, so you miss the bus, causing you to get home ten minutes before your parent-guardian arrives. They find you only just starting to clean when they get home, but they expect the house to be clean already, causing a big argument.

- Think of yourself in both positions.
- How would your guardian feel?
- What arguments would you, as a parent, make?
- How would you feel being yelled at in that situation?
- How would you respond?
- What amicable solution could be reached?
- How could this be prevented in the future?

Conflict Resolution Scenarios: How Will You React?

Exercise 31: Work Conflict

A worker has a part-time job at a local pizzeria and worked there for about six months. The owner had water damage in their home, which caused some financial trouble. At the end of the month, he could not pay the workers but promised to pay them later. How would you react in this scenario if you were the worker? How would you feel? How do you think you would feel if you were the owner? Consider this scenario in depth from both perspectives - of the owner and the worker.

Exercise 32: Friendship Conflict

You have been friends with someone for almost ten years. You buy yourself a brand-new car. You trust your friend who asks if they could borrow the car to fetch their mother from the airport. You say it is okay. On the way to the airport, your friend stops to buy a few things at the store. While your friend is in the store, the car gets stolen. Your friend was only gone for a few minutes and ensured everything was locked.

It wasn't your friend's fault the car got stolen; it is just an unfortunate event.

- How would you feel?
- How would your friend feel?
- Consider scenarios about the situation that could cause the friendship to end. Consider scenarios that could make the friendship stronger.
- What's the worst thing that could happen from your friend's perspective?
- What's the best thing that could happen in this scenario?
- What is the best and worst outcome in this scenario from your perspective?

What would you do if your friend borrowed your car and something terrible happened?

https://www.pexels.com/photo/a-young-woman-behind-the-steering-wheel-6816982/

Dialectical Analysis of Yourself and Relationships

Exercise 33: Internal Conflict Balancing

In a previous exercise, you were asked to make a list of dialectical statements about yourself, like, "I put a hard shell over my feelings, but I am vulnerable." Take the list and explore how those contradictions can work in your favor and how they can be detrimental to you. Go into detail and imagine scenarios where the contradiction could apply in your life.

Exercise 34: Weighing Negativity and Positivity in Relationships

Think about someone you are close to, whether a family member, a friend, or a teacher. Write down everything you love about this person. Write down everything you hate about this person. Now, write down how the things you hate about them benefit your relationship. Then, write down how the things you love about them could be detrimental to you. Consider how there is positive in the negative and negative in the positive.

Exercise 35: Pros and Cons

A great way to better decide is by listing the pros and cons of both situations. Think about two extracurricular activities you would like to participate in. Write a list of pros and cons for each activity. Highlight the best and worst possible outcomes for each activity. Include what you would do in each scenario if the worst possible outcome occurs and if the best possible outcome happens.

Exercise 36: Choices for the Future

After your school career, you must make choices impacting your future in the long-term choices of whether you'll attend college or begin working. Many considerations and factors must play into making this decision.

Here's a mock scenario to address these issues.

- First, write down three possible majors you could choose for college.
- Next, write down three possible fields you could work in straight after high school.
- Now, list the pros and cons of each scenario.
- Next, write down the best and worst possible outcomes for each scenario.
- Write down what external influences will affect your decision and what internal influences, like emotions and perceptions, could affect your decision.

This deep analysis route can help you make many important life choices.

Section 5: Coping with Life's Hurdles

Everyone faces hurdles and obstacles. Life is not about what gets thrown at you; it's about how hard you swing at the curveballs. Your success is 10% about what happens to you and 90% about how you respond to adversity. You may get a bad grade on a test, or you might grow apart from some of your closest friends. These situations aren't pleasurable for anyone, but how you respond will make the difference between being crushed and rising from the ashes.

Life is full of challenges. Hurdles can often derail and have a knock-on impact, spiraling your life into a complete mess. It is crucial to have well-developed coping skills to prevent the tornado from being overwhelmed by challenges. Overcoming obstacles seems impossible at times, but it can be rewarding once you've reached the top of a treacherous mountain. Therefore, the following exercises are practical ways to get through difficult spots without having a total meltdown.

Learning to overcome life's hurdles can stop you from being overwhelmed by challenges.
https://www.pickpik.com/woman-thoughtful-pensive-young-face-caucasian-3473

Exercises to Overcome Hurdles

Exercise 37: Coping with Creativity

Creativity can be helpful as a coping mechanism. If you are confused about how to solve a problem, taking time away from it can bring clarity. Art is a perfect distraction. Go to a park or somewhere scenic and calming in your town. Take a notepad, a pencil, and an eraser. Draw the surrounding scenery. You do not have to be a great artist. Just do the best you can. After spending some time drawing, revisit the problem.

Exercise 38: Distracting Yourself to Focus with Physical Activity

Sometimes, obstacles are mental. This mental strain can manifest when you work hard on something requiring much focus, like a school assignment. You can get it out of your mind with some physical activity. When working on a project and feeling stuck at your desk, do 20-50 push-ups, depending on your fitness level. The physical strain will take your focus off your work for a while so that your mind can refresh.

Exercise 39: Journaling

Keeping a journal is a useful tip for overcoming hurdles.

- Write a journal entry about a challenge you are facing.
- Include why it is a challenge and how you feel about the difficulty.
- If you do not overcome the challenge, write about the worst-case and best-case scenarios.
- Also, write about the best and worst-case scenarios if you *do* overcome the obstacle.

Exercise 40: Music to Escape

Listening to music can help you escape reality.
https://www.pexels.com/photo/cheerful-black-woman-with-earphones-dancing-3800507/

A song can be a two to five-minute escape from reality. Moreover, songs can reflect your emotions or give you encouragement. When working on something challenging, play music in the background or during a thirty-minute workout in the morning. Use upbeat music when you are exercising and see how the impact encourages you.

Exercise 41: The McGregor Method

Your self-talk is central to creating the right mindset to face challenges. The famous UFC fighter, Connor McGregor, is known for hyping himself up for weeks leading up to an MMA fight. Use affirmations to brainwash yourself into crushing challenges. Repeat mantras like, "I will conquer this task," "I am Unstoppable," and "To me, this task is nothing; it is light work."

Exercise 42: Repeat, Repeat, and Repeat

Creating good daily habits can help you when challenges occur. Habits are created through repetition. Exercising for one hour every morning helps you prepare for challenges. Pushing yourself to your physical limits every morning can create an attitude of overcoming obstacles daily. You are prepping your mind for difficulty so you do not fold under pressure.

Exercise 43: Limiting Screen Time

Too much screen time can make you unproductive and cause procrastination. Furthermore, blue light before bedtime messes with your sleep cycle. Low-quality sleep and procrastination amplify challenges due to bad time management. Write down the number of hours you will spend in front of a screen daily (most smartphones have screen time trackers) and ensure you follow your schedule. Also, shut off all technology at least an hour before bed.

Exercise 44: Starting a Hobby

Starting a hobby is another helpful distraction in dealing with challenges. Think about something you would like to learn for fun, like knitting or coding. Check YouTube and look up videos for beginners on your chosen activity. Put thirty minutes aside every day to practice this skill. It will give you something to take your mind off the constant pressure you face.

Exercise 45: Nighttime Self-Care Routine

Self-care is the process of nurturing yourself. It is like a refueling station where you refill your energy to complete the tasks of the day or week. Develop a nighttime cleansing ritual, including face scrubs, exfoliators, and moisturizers. You can also include hair care products. The ritual should be no longer than 15 minutes and should be done just before bed. When applying your products, visualize how they are refueling you.

Exercise 46: Visualization

Visualization is a mental activity that can propel you past your limitations. When you feel overwhelmed by a specific task, visualize yourself conquering the task. Go into detail with your visualization. Think about how you will feel, what you will say, and how it will smell and look. It gives you a clear picture of the goal you are working toward.

Exercise 47: Hiking For Clarity

Few things clear the mind quite like getting out into nature. Google nature reserves in your area. Most nature reserves have hiking trails, so enjoy hiking with some friends. It helps with obstacles because it is relaxing, and you will feel accomplished at the end of a hike.

Exercise 48: Ask For Help

There is no shame in asking for help. When you feel overwhelmed, reach out to your social circle. One obstacle overcome with social support is better grades. Form a study group with classmates. You do not have to meet up if it is not possible. Technology facilitates long-distance meetings, so set up a Zoom study group. Meet every day for an hour to work on one or two shared subjects.

Exercise 49: Yoga

Yoga can help you relieve stress.

https://www.pexels.com/photo/photo-of-woman-in-orange-tank-top-and-black-pants-striking-a-yoga-pose-outdoors-3658399/

Yoga helps relieve stress so you can maintain a clearer mind to deal with your life hurdles. Search for 10-minute yoga videos on YouTube. The combination of stretching and mindful breathing can be very relaxing. Make time to do one ten-minute yoga flow daily.

Section 6: Expressing Yourself and Navigating Relationships

Communication is a science. Interpersonal relationships are largely based on the science of communication. The communication cycle starts with the message's sender. The message passes through a channel; it could be technology or a biological vehicle like your voice. The receiver gets the messages, decodes them according to their perceptions, and then provides feedback. The ability to apply certain skills at all levels of the communication cycle allows for better self-expression and building social cohesion to maintain healthy relationships.

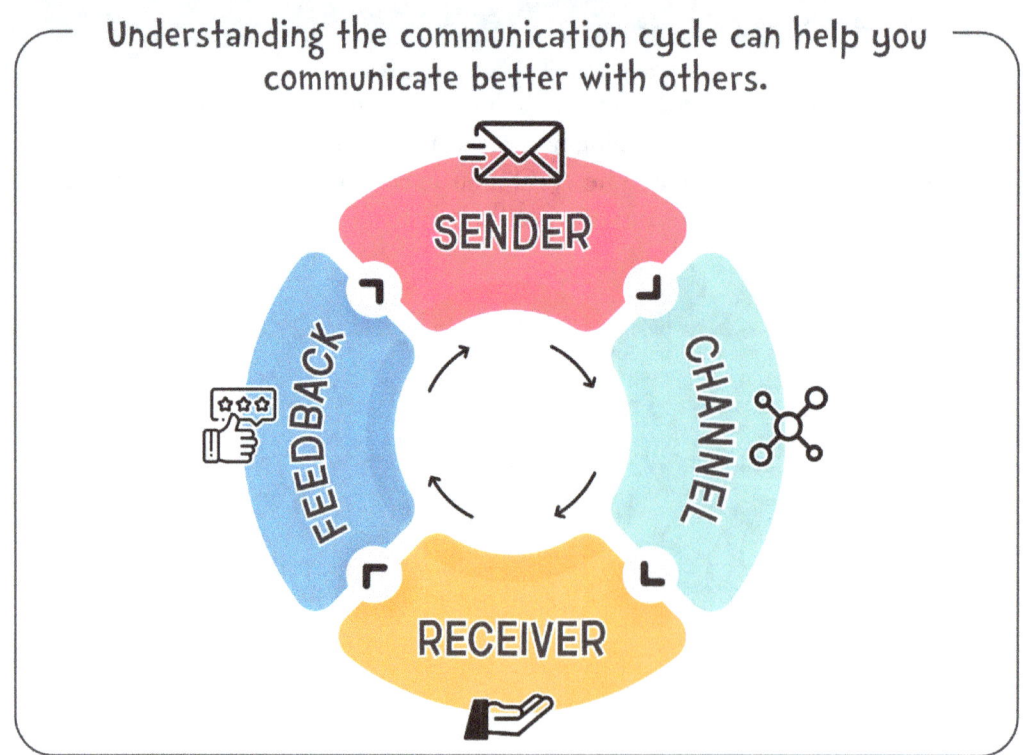

Understanding the communication cycle can help you communicate better with others.

5 Techniques to Help with Self-Expression

Exercise 50: Today I Fell Like...

It can be intimidating to express yourself openly. One tip for learning to express yourself is to choose three people you will inform about your feelings once daily. Start your sentence with, "Today I feel like 'blank' because of ..."

Exercise 51: Karaoke For Self-Expression

Next time you are listening to music, sing along passionately. Embodying the lyrics of a song can help with self-expression.

Exercise 52: Move Your Body

Learning to dance can help you tap into using your body for self-expression. Google dance tutorials and learn a few steps.

Exercise 53: Talk To Yourself, It's Not Crazy

Talking to yourself can help you express yourself freely.
https://www.pexels.com/photo/photo-of-woman-looking-at-the-mirror-774866/

Talking to yourself seems crazy to some, but it is perfect for learning self-expression freely. Look in the mirror and ask yourself questions. Maintain eye contact with your reflection and answer the questions.

Exercise 54: The Introduction Game

A fun practice for introducing a new group is having everybody state their names. After they say their names, they must make a sound and body movement expressing how they feel. Everyone in the group then mimics the sound and movement before moving on to the next person.

How to Make and Maintain Healthy Relationships

Exercise 55: Ask Your Parents How They Feel

Healthy relationships begin with honesty and considering other people's feelings. Practice asking your parents how they feel each evening at dinner.

Exercise 56: Listen Attentively

Listening is an important part of building relationships. One technique you can apply to listen better is to repeat what the person says back to them in your own words. For example, say, "Do you mean...?" or "Do I understand you correctly...?"

Exercise 57: Set Your Boundaries

Boundaries are an important part of relationships. Be firm when you say no. Do not use wobbly denials like "Maybe another time," "I'll think about it," or "Not right now" when you mean no.

Exercise 58: Compliments Matter

Being honest about your positive feelings helps strengthen relationships. Practice complimenting one person daily and telling them why they are important to you.

Exercise 59: Defining Your Relationships

Defining a relationship clearly can work wonders. Talk to a friend or family and ask them what they want from their relationship with you. Tell them what you expect of them and discuss the details openly.

Conflict Resolution Baby Steps

Exercise 60: Step Away From the Fight

Conflict can be intimidating – especially if you are conflict-avoidant. Sometimes, taking some time away from the conflict is helpful. When an argument is unproductive, request some space and revisit the argument later.

Exercise 61: Switch the Roles

Seeing things from another person's view can be helpful. When you can reflect on a conflict, imagine yourself in the other person's shoes.

Write about what it would be like to be someone you do not get along with.

Exercise 62: State Your Feelings

When in a conflict, communicate your feelings clearly. Start sentences with, "When you said or did that, I felt like this because of..."

Section 7: Emotional Outbursts and How to Control Them

It is common for teenagers to experience emotional outbursts occasionally. These outbursts can be caused by the pressure and increased responsibility of entering adulthood. Moreover, hormonal changes profoundly influence mood and temperance. Although emotional outbursts are part of being a teenager, the consequences of exhibiting extreme emotion could adversely impact your social life and mental health. Therefore, learning to control emotional outbursts is crucial.

Having emotional outbursts and difficult days is completely fine. Losing it does not mean you are a terrible person. Nobody is completely put together all the time. The space to lose grip of yourself is needed for you to experience the full expression of being a human. Do not beat yourself up for not being perfectly put together. The cracks on the surface *make you unique.*

Teenagers are likely to have emotional outbursts.
https://www.pexels.com/photo/woman-holding-her-head-2128817/

This chapter equips you with the skills and techniques to manage emotional outbursts and calm down.

Dealing with Emotional Outbursts

Exercise 63: Understanding Your Emotional Intensity

When you have an emotional outburst, your emotions are at the highest level on the emotional intensity scale.

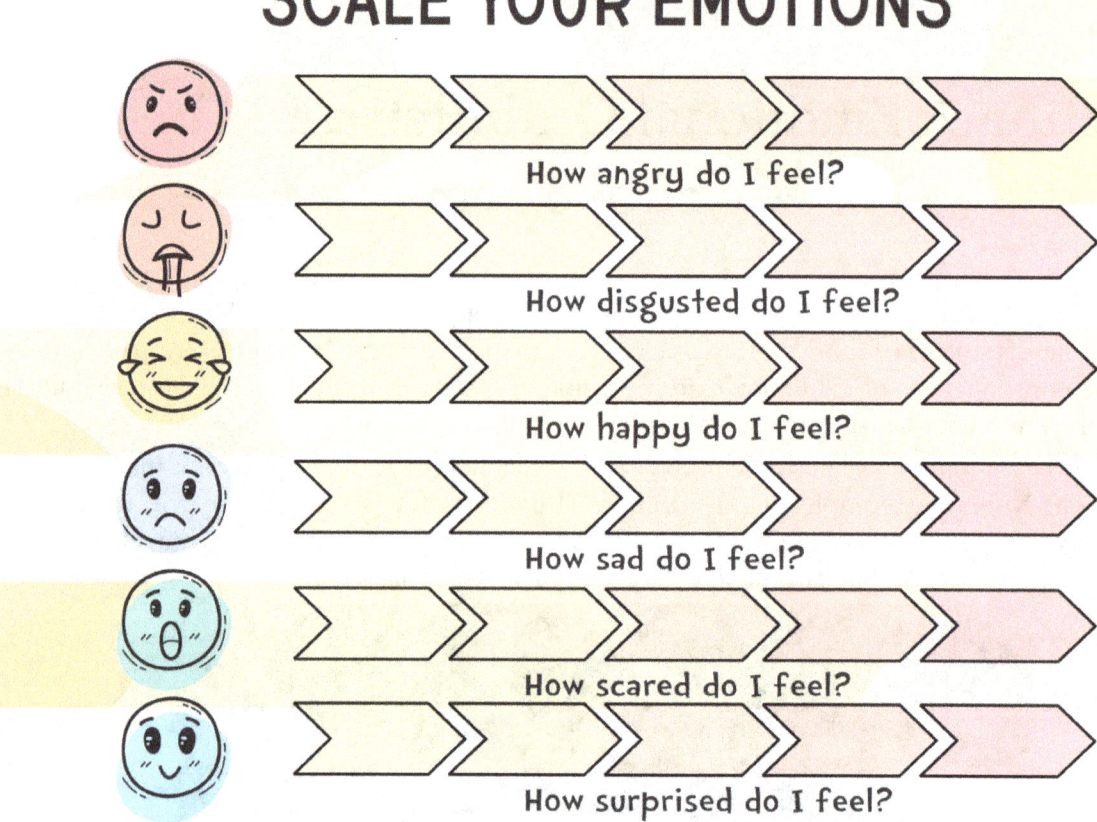

To address this outburst, you must ask yourself:

- Why am I experiencing this emotion with such intensity?
- What triggered this emotional response?
- How can I manage this emotional response?
- How was I feeling before the outburst?

Exercise 64: Trigger Awareness

Before an emotional outburst occurs, some signs indicate it is about to happen. Self-awareness can help you identify the triggers and emotions leading to an outburst.

- Reflect on an emotional outburst you've had in the past.

- Focus on how you felt at that moment. Could you feel the intensity building up, or was it sudden?

Exercise 65: Fidget Away Your Negativity

Self-soothing can help prevent emotional outbursts or control your emotions better. Texture can be a useful way to self-soothe.

- Find a small toy or object that feels good to the touch. For instance, a stress ball, a fidget toy, or anything else that fits into your palm.
- When you feel aggravated, fidget with this toy and focus on the textures to calm down.

This toy can be carried wherever you go, so ensure you choose a portable object that fits into a pocket or a purse.

Having a stress toy to release tension is a great way to deal with intrusive thoughts.
https://www.pexels.com/photo/cool-teen-girl-with-spring-toy-3808981/

Exercise 66: Sound Healing

Sound is another brilliant self-soothing tool. When you feel you are about to explode, listen to calming music for a while. Take deep breaths while you let the music relax you. You could take the opposite approach and listen to aggressive music if you need something to relate to your feelings. Music stimulates various brainwaves, allowing you to exit the cycles that may be causing extreme emotional behavior. Being trapped in a certain mindset can become unhealthy.

Exercise 67: Finding the Root Cause

Sometimes, what triggered the outburst is not the cause. Take about thirty minutes to reflect on your emotions. Dig deep and explore the corners of your mind. You might find underlying, suppressed feelings you have not dealt with. Consider how you have felt, not only the specific moment of the outburst. Your overall mood over an extended period could be the reason for an emotional outburst at that moment. Tracking your mood could reveal the origins of an outburst.

Exercise 68: How Do Your Emotions Feel?

Searching your body for your feelings is a technique to help develop self-awareness. Think about something that makes you angry. Now feel where you feel the sensation in your body. For example, you may feel your chest tightening or your head throbbing. Use breathing techniques to relieve the negativity from that body area.

Exercise 69: Locating the Position of the Emotion

Think about something that makes you sad. Pay attention to where the feeling is located in your body. Compare it to how you feel when angry and observe the differences. You will gain deeper insight into your emotions. Different feelings create varying sensations in the body, so being more aware of these sensations can help you navigate your feelings better.

Exercise 70: Frustration Buster

Sometimes, emotional outbursts are triggered due to the inability to solve a problem effectively.

- Think about an issue that has left you frustrated in the past.
- Get a notebook and brainstorm ways to solve the problem.
- Do not be judgmental. Write down every idea, even if it seems silly.

Letting your mind flow freely to solve problems can stimulate creativity.

Brainstorming is another effective way to get your thoughts in order and find solutions to your problems.

https://www.pxfuel.com/en/free-photo-jnnhp

Exercise 71: Accurately Defining Problems

Be specific in defining your problems. For example, define what is wrong with the car instead of saying a car is broken. There could be an issue with the brakes, or the ignition may be faulty. If you have a clearly defined problem, developing a targeted solution makes it easier. Thinking about things too broadly can sometimes be a hindrance. Zooming into a problem can create a viewpoint where solutions come more easily.

Exercise 72: Get Some Space

When an emotional outburst happens, sometimes all that is needed is some space.

- When angry, overwhelmed, or annoyed, walk away.
- Once some distance is created, lay down flat or remove your shoes to feel grounded.
- Take a few deep breaths and focus on your breathing - an overly emotional state speeds up your breathing.
- Once your breath is calmed, revisit the situation.

Exercise 73: Communicate Your Feelings

When overwhelmed, frustrated, or annoyed, communicate your feelings to those around you. Be specific about what and why it is triggering you. It allows for a dialogue to open from which conflict resolution can occur. Not everybody will always be receptive to open communication, but it lets you inform people where you stand. Keeping feelings hidden is not always advisable. People could be feeling the same as you, which allows bonding.

Exercise 74: Visualize Yourself to Stability

Visualization can help with emotional control and distress tolerance.

- Sit down and close your eyes.
- Take a few deep breaths.
- Imagine yourself in a place that brings you joy.
- Be vivid and include details like sights, sounds, smells, and textures.

You can always escape into your mind when necessary. Your imagination is one of the greatest assets for distress tolerance and emotional regulation.

Exercise 75: Night Time Feelings Recap

Sit on the edge of your bed before you sleep and think about the feelings that stood out for the day. Take note of what was happening and your thoughts. This analysis can be awareness of your emotional state daily. This daily checking in with yourself ensures no emotions sneak up on you unexpectedly because you remain in tune with your inner world. Furthermore, it is a practice that does not take much time, and you can go to bed after dealing with your stress.

Section 8: Compassion, Kindness, and Mental Health

Feeling understood is a significant contributor to maintaining your well-being. People who feel understood are usually happier and experience more satisfaction in daily life. The cornerstones of feeling understood are kindness and compassion. Therefore, showing kindness and compassion in various social interactions will build stronger interpersonal relationships.

Compassion can help you build stronger relationships.
https://www.pexels.com/photo/person-holding-heart-shaped-cut-out-1820525/

Your Road to Stronger Relationships

Exercise 76: Positive Relationship Affirmations

Kindness and compassion for others begin with kindness and compassion toward yourself. This self-compassion and self-kindness can be cultivated in meditation - sit quietly and comfortably, take a few deep breaths, and repeat the affirmations:

- *I am loved.*
- *I am healthy.*
- *I am safe.*
- *I am at ease.*

Exercise 77: Gratitude Journal

Keep a gratitude journal.

- Write down three things you are grateful for in your life right now.
- Then, write down three people you are grateful for.
- Now, write down three events in your past that you are grateful for because they significantly contributed to positive parts of yourself right now.

Exercise 78: Mindful Eating

Practicing self-care can grow compassion for yourself and others. No self-care is as primal and fundamental as eating. Each week, prepare a dish you enjoy. Take your time preparing it and get lost in the moment. Mindfully eat the meal as you express gratitude to yourself.

Exercise 79: Empathy Builder

Building empathy helps grow compassion and kindness.

- Write down one important person in your life.
- Imagine yourself in their shoes. Imagine their experiences and the emotions they go through.
- Go into detail with the imagery and allow yourself to get carried away within the scenarios you paint in your mind.

Exercise 80: Random Acts of Kindness

You can spread compassion and show empathy by doing random acts of kindness. This action can include giving money to a homeless person or holding the door open for somebody. Make it part of your daily mission to complete at least three random acts of kindness daily.

Volunteer work and random acts of kindness will give you a sense of purpose and empathy towards others.
https://pxhere.com/en/photo/1557065

Exercise 81: Take It Easy

It is easy to be hard on yourself. Your ambitions and goals drive you to hold yourself to a high standard. However, making mistakes is a part of being human. People find it easier to give others some leeway but drive down hard on themselves to emphasize their inadequacies. Practice self-forgiveness and mercy because beating yourself up constantly seldom yields positive results.

- Write down a time that you made a mistake. When you write down your mistake, start the sentence with "I am still worthy of love, respect, and compassion even though I..."

- Write a sentence to forgive yourself. Structure the sentence like this, "I forgive myself for...because..."

Exercise 82: Social Media Reconfiguring

Compassion can also be fine-tuned through your social media habits. The distance and anonymity the internet facilitates can often encourage the lowest, vindictive behavior in people. Challenge yourself to respond kindly to people on your social media pages or in your internet comments. Your positivity will be rewarded by the way people respond to you.

Exercise 83: Spend Time With Others

Self-isolation can be a killer of compassion. If you get into a space of wanting to be alone all the time, consider going out and meeting up with friends or family. Even within your household, share space with your mom, dad, or siblings instead of staying hauled up in your room. Interacting with people more often gives you varying perspectives, which could help you understand people better. You can learn to be kinder and more compassionate from this understanding of social connection.

Exercise 84: Release It Now

To practice self-compassion, you can engage in releasing statements. These statements are similar to positive affirmations but permit you to experience negativity.

For example, you may have become angry at someone and feel very bad about it. Release that emotion with forgiveness by affirming, "It is okay that I got angry. I am a person, so it is normal to experience a vast array of emotions."

Exercise 85: Daily Compassion Challenge

Compassion and kindness begin at home.

- Give yourself a daily challenge to show kindness to those you live with.
- Set a goal of doing three kinds of things each day in your home. These acts do not have to be complicated.
- It could be making your mother a cup of tea when she gets home from work without her having to ask.

Exercise 86: Destroying Jealously

Celebrate with your peers for their accomplishments. Competition is healthy, so it is perfectly normal to want to finish ahead of everybody else. However, you cannot allow your competitive edge to grow into envy. Jealousy could result in you treating people horribly, which will hurt your interpersonal connections. Therefore, allow yourself to celebrate others' accomplishments and share their joy.

Exercise 87: You Are Not Alone

Occasionally, times will arise when you feel isolated. In these moments, compassion can be a substantial tool to dig yourself out of a rut. Remind yourself that you are not the only one experiencing adversity. People are going through what you are experiencing right now. So, realigning your mind to think of yourself in relation to others helps alleviate loneliness.

Exercise 88: Be Encouraging

Helping others is great. However, you may not be capable of helping others due to various reasons like time or a lack of expertise. You can grow your compassion and strengthen your relationships by being encouraging. Practice supportive language to uplift your friends and family. For example, "You will get through this. I've seen you beat challenges like this many times."

Reflection

Think about your flaws. How do your flaws contribute to making you a unique person? Is there any good that comes from your flaws? Some people do not have any arms or legs, but they know how to swim well enough to push against strong ocean currents. How can overcoming your flaws to achieve your goals help you grow as a person?

Section 9: Using DBT to Build Social Skills

As a social species, humans find validation through relationships. DBT can help you develop the social skills to build strong relationships. The validation felt within the context of relationships contributes to self-esteem and confidence, which significantly impacts your well-being and mental health.

Humans tend to find validation through relationships
https://www.pexels.com/photo/young-couple-in-city-at-night-246367/

DEAR MAN Interpersonal Skill

The primary skill for interpersonal development and building social skills in DBT is the DEAR MAN method. The following exercises will walk you through the method and show you how to use it.

Exercise 89: D in DEARMAN

D EARMAN

The D in DEAR MAN stands for *describe*. During communication, describe to the person what is occurring. It will ensure everyone is on the same page. Practice explicitly stating what you think is happening in an interaction when there could be misunderstandings or lack of clarity.

Exercise 90: E in DEARMAN

D **E** ARMAN

The E in DEAR MAN stands for *express*. Once you have described the situation, express emotions, perceptions, or opinions during the exchanges. Try incorporating the words "I feel like," "I think that," or "This makes me feel like" into your vocabulary.

Exercise 91: A in DEARMAN

DE **A** RMAN

The A in DEAR MAN stands for *assert*. Asserting yourself is about establishing strong boundaries. You cannot help everybody or fulfill everybody's needs. As a person, you are limited and do not want to become a doormat everyone walks all over. Practice saying no to your peers when they ask you to do things you are uncomfortable with or participate in activities you do not want to join in. Be firm with your no because they might try to convince you otherwise.

Exercise 92: R in DEARMAN

DEA **R** MAN

The R in DEAR MAN stands for **reinforce**. In communication, reinforcing means rewarding positive responses and presenting consequences for negative responses. Try smiling when someone says something you like or agree with. When someone says something you are uncomfortable with, make it known with a frown or say, "I did not like what you said because..."

Exercise 93: M in DEARMAN

D E A R M(M)A N

The M in DEAR MAN stands for *mindful*. Consistently considering others' feelings is crucial for building healthy relationships. Use the prompts, "How did that make you feel?" or "What do you think about that?" to show people you care about their feelings.

Exercise 94: A in DEARMAN

D E A R M(A) N

The A in DEAR MAN stands for *appear*. How you present yourself to the world impacts how you are received. There is a reason PR companies say "image is everything." Confidence is the best way to get your communication taken seriously. Stand tall with your shoulders back when talking to someone. It is also helpful to maintain eye contact. Being unable to hold eye contact shows you are shy or uncomfortable with yourself. This insecure image is not what you want to be perceived as.

Exercise 95: N in DEARMAN

D E A R M A(N)

The N in DEAR MAN stands for *negotiation*. As much as asserting yourself and establishing boundaries are important, you must bend a little now and then. Common ground cannot be found if you are immovable and stubborn. Practice negotiation using conversational prompts like, "How can we come to a compromise?" or "If I do this for you, will you do that for me?"

Exercise 96: Staring Contest

Before you can communicate well, you must be comfortable with communication. This exercise is especially helpful if you are a shy person. Do a staring contest with a trusted friend or family member. It will get you comfortable with maintaining eye contact when speaking to people.

Exercise 97: Build A Story

A game that can be played with friends to strengthen bonds and build communication skills is improvisational storytelling. Sit in a circle with your friends or family. Each person takes a turn to contribute to a story. However, each person can only say one word. It is a fun way to break the tension and become comfortable with people.

Exercise 98: Join Social Clubs

If you have not joined any social clubs or do not participate in extracurricular activities, it is advisable to do so. Social clubs and team sports help develop social skills. A shared common interest is a powerful tool for bonding. So, consider your interests and join groups aligning with those interests.

Exercise 99: Maps of Analysis

With a group of close friends, draw up mind maps of self-analysis. Include your interests, fears, dreams, goals, and what is most meaningful in your life. Exchange these mind maps with your friends or peers and ask one another questions about what you wrote.

Exercise 100: Charity

Join a weekend charity program. If you look up charitable organizations in your area, you will realize they are always seeking volunteers. In these programs, you will be exposed to many people with varying perspectives from yours. These programs can help you build better social skills.

Exercise 101: Public Speaking and Debate

Join a debate team or participate in public speaking. This activity allows you to find your voice and overcome your nervousness by communicating. Moreover, debating and public speaking allows you to think through what you say more thoroughly, helping you in social situations. If there are no debate teams or public speaking clubs close to you, try posting videos of yourself talking online.

Section 10: Accountability Quiz

You have read and practiced the exercises in this book. Now, take it a step further and evaluate your growth and understanding by taking this accountability quiz. Where you feel unconfident in your responses, revise the related section for better clarity.

1. Which mindfulness practices have you applied this week, and how did they help you improve your daily experiences?

2. How many mindfulness walks have you taken this week? Why did you take those walks? If you have taken any mindfulness walks, why haven't you?

3. Have you felt negative emotions this week? Which strategies from the workbook did you apply for emotional regulation or to address your distress?

4. Write down what you are feeling right now and rate how positive or negative your emotions are.

5. Did you apply any of the communication skills outlined in the workbook? How did these techniques help you? What were the challenges you faced while trying to implement these communication techniques?

6. Have you used the DEAR MAN technique this week? How did you use it?

7. Have you used any of the mentioned dialectical thinking techniques to help balance opposing thoughts or emotions this week? How did applying dialectics help you?

8. Write down affirmations that can uplift you from any doubts or anxieties you currently have. Say them out loud seven times.

9. After reading this workbook, have you set goals and drafted a detailed plan with daily instructions to achieve your goals?

10. Which daily goals have you achieved today?

11. Have you asked anybody for help with the obstacles you encountered?

12. Since reading this workbook, have you become angry or frustrated? What techniques did you use to examine your anger and address it effectively?

13. Slow down and take seven deep breaths. How does your body feel? Which emotions can you recognize coming up?

14. Are you keeping a daily journal? How has journaling impacted your life?

15. Who have you asked how they feel this week? If you haven't asked anybody, why?

Thank You Message

Thank you for purchasing this book but, more importantly, for applying the exercises within its page. The world is experiencing a mental health crisis, especially among the younger population. So, taking the steps to work on your mental health is encouraging and inspiring. The book's deepest hope is that you continue with DBT techniques and philosophies to maximize your personal growth through emotional regulation, mindfulness, distress tolerance, and interpersonal effectiveness. By taking this journey, you are setting yourself up for success, so with gratitude, you are encouraged to diligently continue moving forward with the newly found outlook this workbook provided. Keep pushing forward and taking your mental health seriously.

Check out another book in the series

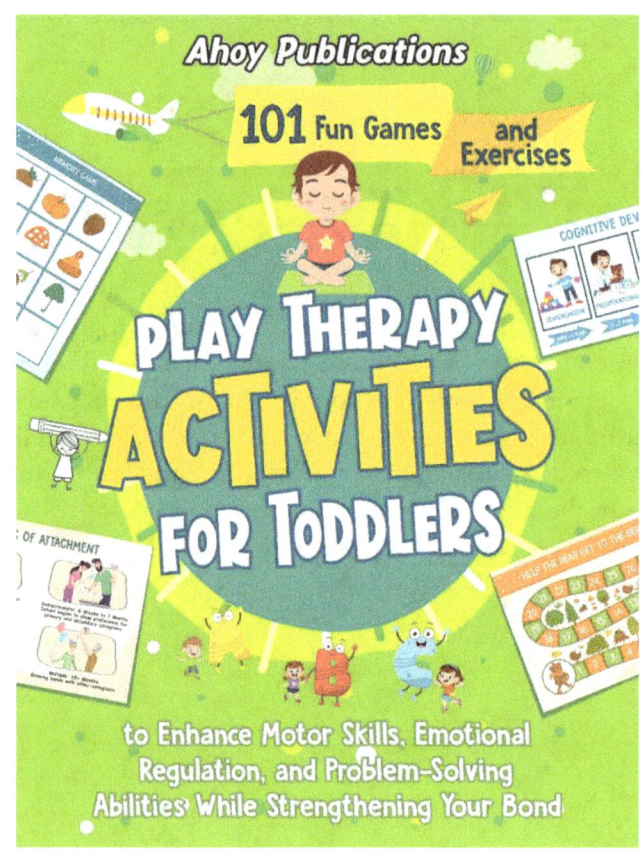

References

Cole, C. (2019, December 9). Dialectical behavior therapy (DBT) - part 2 - regulating your emotions has radical rewards. The Center for Family Transformation. https://www.familytransformation.com/2019/12/09/dialectical-behavior-therapy-dbt-part-2-regulating-your-emotions-has-radical-rewards/

Courtney E. Ackerman, M. A. (2017, January 18). 21 mindfulness exercises & activities for adults (+ PDF). Positivepsychology.com. https://positivepsychology.com/mindfulness-exercises-techniques-activities/

Courtney E. Ackerman, M. A. (2017, March 14). 20 DBT worksheets and dialectical Behavior Therapy skills. Positivepsychology.com. https://positivepsychology.com/dbt-dialectical-behavior-therapy/

DBT interpersonal effectiveness skills: The guide to healthy relationships. (2017, August 18). Sunrise Residential Treatment Center. https://sunrisertc.com/interpersonal-effectiveness/

Fassbinder, E., Schweiger, U., Martius, D., Brand-de Wilde, O., & Arntz, A. (2016). Emotion regulation in schema therapy and dialectical behavior therapy. Frontiers in Psychology, 7, 1373. https://doi.org/10.3389/fpsyg.2016.01373

Gattig, N. (n.d.). 18 effective strategies to improve your communication skills. Betterup.com. https://www.betterup.com/blog/effective-strategies-to-improve-your-communication-skills

Hoshaw, C. (2021, April 16). Mindfulness activities: Easy mindfulness exercises for any age. Healthline. https://www.healthline.com/health/mind-body/mindfulness-activities

Kendra Cherry, M. (2009, March 3). What is cognitive behavioral therapy (CBT)? Verywell Mind. https://www.verywellmind.com/what-is-cognitive-behavior-therapy-2795747

Kendra Cherry, M. (2021, October 31). What Is Compassion? Verywell Mind. https://www.verywellmind.com/what-is-compassion-5207366

Li, E. (N.d.). Pexels.com. https://www.pexels.com/photo/teen-boy-doing-yoga-in-lotus-position-7241488/

Linehan, M. (n.d.). DEAR MAN skill. Dialectical Behavior Therapy (DBT) Tools; JW-Designs. https://dbt.tools/interpersonal_effectiveness/dear-man.php

Linehan, M. (n.d.). Interpersonal effectiveness skills. Dialectical Behavior Therapy (DBT) Tools; JW-Designs. https://dbt.tools/interpersonal_effectiveness/index.php

Linehan, M. M., & Wilks, C. R. (2015). The course and evolution of dialectical behavior therapy. American Journal of Psychotherapy, 69(2), 97–110. https://doi.org/10.1176/appi.psychotherapy.2015.69.2.97

Lun, J., Kesebir, S., & Oishi, S. (2008). On feeling understood and feeling well: The role of interdependence. Journal of Research in Personality, 42(6), 1623–1628. https://doi.org/10.1016/j.jrp.2008.06.009

Moore, C. (2019, June 2). How to practice self-compassion: 8 techniques and tips. Positivepsychology.com.

https://positivepsychology.com/how-to-practice-self-compassion/

Nunez, K., & Romanoff, S. (2023, April 27). 7 simple mindfulness exercises that can reduce stress and anxiety. SELF. https://www.self.com/story/best-mindfulness-exercises

Riiderhof, A. (N.d.). Pixabay.com. https://pixabay.com/illustrations/mandala-lines-pattern-form-line-1803545/

Schimelpfening, N. (2007, October 29). Dialectical behavior therapy (DBT): Definition, techniques, and benefits. Verywell Mind. https://www.verywellmind.com/dialectical-behavior-therapy-1067402

Sutton, J. (2022, January 28). How to use mindfulness therapy for anxiety: 15 exercises. Positivepsychology.com. https://positivepsychology.com/mindfulness-for-anxiety

www.ingramcontent.com/pod-product-compliance
Lightning Source LLC
Chambersburg PA
CBHW081005140626
46546CB00019B/3442

* 9 7 8 1 9 6 1 2 1 7 2 9 4 *